KINGFISHER
READERS

Sun, Moon and Stars

Hannah Wilson

KINGFISHER

First published 2014 by Kingfisher
an imprint of Macmillan Children's Books
a division of Macmillan Publishers Limited
20 New Wharf Road, London N1 9RR
Basingstoke and Oxford
Associated companies throughout the world
www.panmacmillan.com

Series editor: Polly Goodman
Literacy consultant: Hilary Horton

ISBN: 978-0-7534-3668-4
Copyright © Macmillan Publishers Ltd 2014

1 3 5 7 9 8 6 4 2

1TR/0913/WKT/UG/105MA

A CIP catalogue record for this book is available from
the British Library.

Printed in China

Picture credits
The Publisher would like to thank the following for permission to reproduce their material.
Every care has been taken to trace copyright holders. However, if there have been unintentional
omissions or failure to trace copyright holders, we apologise and will, if informed, endeavour
to make corrections in any future edition.

Top = t; Bottom = b; Centre = c; Left = l; Right = r
Cover Shutterstock/Johan Swanepoel/Paul Paladin; Pages 4l Shutterstock/Elena Schweitzer; 4r Shutterstock/
Elenamiv; 5 Science Photo Library/David Nunuk; 6 Shutterstock/PaulPaladin; 7t&b Shutterstock/sebikus;
8–9 KF Archive; 10 Shutterstock/liseykina; 11t Shutterstock/Cristian Zamfir; 11b Shutterstock/tadamichi;
12 Shutterstock/USBFCO; 13 KF Archive; 14 Shutterstock/Richard Schramm; 15 KF Archive; 16 Shutterstock/
Kirschner; 17 Shutterstock/MarcelClemens; 18–19 Shutterstock/PavleMarjanovic; 20 Shutterstock/G. K.;
21 Science Photo Library/Andrzej Wojcicki; 22 KF Archive; 23 KF Archive; 24–25 KF Archive; 26 Science Photo
Library/Julian Baum; 27 Science Photo Library/Mark Garlick; 28t Corbis/ClassicStock/H. Armstrong;
28b KF Archive; 29 KF Archive; 30t KF Archive; 30b KF Archive; 31 KF Archive.

Contents

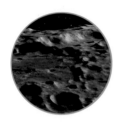

The sky above

Look up at the sky. Is it daytime?
Is the Sun shining? Perhaps it is
night-time. Can you see the Moon
or stars?

The Sun, Moon and stars are very,
very far away. They look tiny, but
really they are huge. What are they
made of? What do they look like
close up? Let's find out!

Earth and space

We live on a **planet** called Earth. We see the Sun, Moon and stars from here. Earth travels around the Sun in **space**.

Sun

Earth

Moon

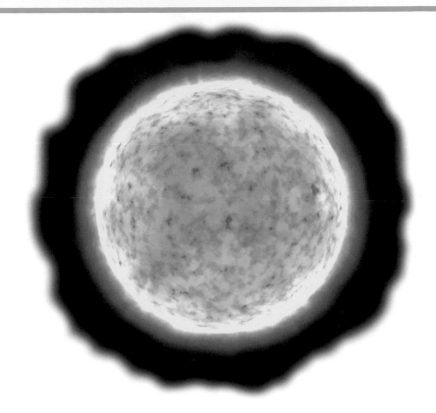

The Sun is a star. There are billions of other stars like the Sun.

The Moon is a ball of rock that travels around Earth.

Sun

The Sun is a star. It is a giant ball of very hot, glowing **gas**. The Sun is so large that it pulls planets towards it.

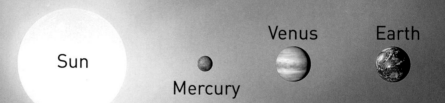

Sun

Mercury

Venus

Earth

Earth and seven other planets travel around the Sun. The Sun and these planets are our **Solar System**.

Mars

Jupiter

Saturn

Uranus

Neptune

Heat and light

The Sun heats Earth and its oceans. This keeps our planet warm enough for animals and plants to live.

Some animals lie in the sunshine to get **energy**. This lizard is sunbathing.

The Sun gives light to Earth and stops it from being dark. Plants turn the light into energy for growing.

Night and day

Why is the sky light in the day and dark at night?

Earth spins on an imaginary stick called an axis. Imagine a pencil stuck through the middle of a spinning orange.

Sun

Day happens when one side of Earth faces the Sun. Night happens when it faces away.

It takes 24 hours for Earth to spin around once. That is why each day lasts for 24 hours, and includes daytime and night-time.

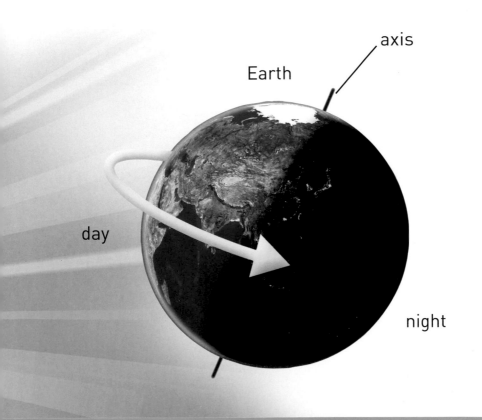

axis

Earth

day

night

Seasons

spring summer

autumn winter

Many parts of Earth have **seasons** called spring, summer, autumn and winter. In summer it is warmer and drier. In winter it is wetter and cooler.

Earth takes one year to travel around the Sun. This journey causes the seasons.

The parts of Earth leaning towards the Sun have summer. The parts that lean away have winter.

summer

winter

Moon

A moon is a ball of rock that travels around a planet. Earth has only one moon, but Mars has two. Jupiter has more than 60 moons!

Jupiter

moons

Earth

Moon

Our Moon is a dry, rocky place
with no wind or rain. Plants and
animals cannot live there.

Moon shapes

The Moon shines at night because light from the Sun bounces off it.

crescent moon

full moon

The Sun's light bounces off different parts of the Moon as it travels around Earth. So different parts of the Moon shine at different times.

A shining, thin curve is called a crescent moon. A complete circle is called a full moon.

crescent moon

On the surface

plains

mountains

Look closely at the Moon on a
clear night. Can you see some dark
patches? These are vast, flat **plains**.

The light patches are mountains and the rings are craters. A crater is a dent that formed when a giant rock crashed into the Moon long ago.

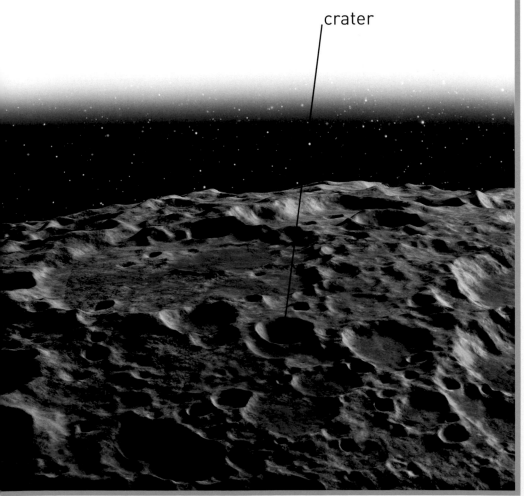

crater

Trip to the Moon

Astronauts travelled to the Moon for the first time in 1969. A huge rocket blasted them into space.

Astronauts are lighter on the Moon so they bounce when they walk. Their footprints will last for millions of years because there is no wind or rain to destroy them!

Stars

Look up into the sky on a clear night. Can you see a milky white stripe?

This is the Milky Way galaxy. A galaxy is a group of stars.

The Sun is just one of billions of stars in the Milky Way. Each star shines because it is a glowing ball of gas like the Sun.

Star colours

The Sun looks yellow or orange, but other stars can be different colours. Some stars are red. They are called red dwarfs. They are smaller and cooler than our Sun.

Some huge stars are blue. They are called blue giants. They are a thousand times larger than the Sun, and much hotter.

Star gazing

Stars, moons and planets are so far away that they look tiny. People use **telescopes** to see them more closely. There are small telescopes that you can use. There are also huge telescopes on remote islands for scientists.

There are even telescopes in space. The Hubble Space Telescope has been taking photographs for more than 20 years!

Star patterns

A constellation is a pattern of stars. Imagine drawing lines to join up the stars and form a picture. The Pegasus constellation looks like a flying horse and the Great Bear constellation looks like a bear.

There are maps showing all the constellations. Can you see Pegasus and the Great Bear on this one?

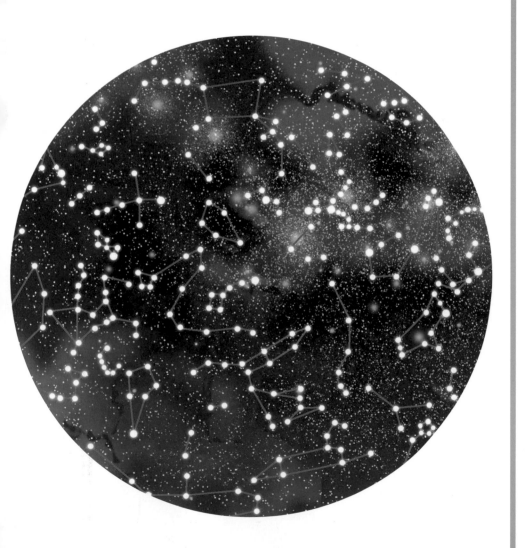

Glossary

astronaut a person who travels into space

energy the power needed to do an activity, such as moving or growing

gas a substance that is neither solid nor liquid

plain a large, flat area of land

planet a large, ball-shaped object that travels around a star in space

season a time of year with certain weather patterns

Solar System the Sun and all the space objects that travel around it

space the vast region beyond Earth's sky

telescope an instrument that shows distant objects more clearly